THE REST IS ~~CENSORED~~

K. LORRAINE GRAHAM

The Rest Is Censored

Second Edition

Design & composition: Shanna Compton, shannacompton.com
Cover art: Larissa Greer, cargocollective.com/larissaeringreer

Published by Bloof Books
PO Box 326
Lambertville NJ 08530
www.bloofbooks.com

Member of CLMP

Bloof Books are printed in the USA by Bookmobile and Spencer Printing. Booksellers, libraries, and other institutions may order direct from us by contacting sales@bloofbooks.com. POD copies are distributed via Ingram, Baker & Taylor, and other wholesalers. Individuals may purchase our books direct from our website, from online retailers such as Amazon.com, or request them from their favorite bookstores.

Please support your local independent bookseller whenever possible.

ISBN-13: 978-0-9965868-3-2
ISBN-10: 0-9965868-3-0

1. American poetry—21st century. 2. Poets, American—21st century.

∞ This paper meets the requirements of ANSI/NISO Z39.48-1992

Contents

ONE

9 Today I objectify
10 The history of history as naked women
11 Too boring to continue
12 Lay words on a page sounds like sex
13 Sit next to someone
14 The woman in the wig
15 A 70s horror movie without the movie
16 The bus driver stops
17 Not because of tacos de birria
18 Black Friday shopping death
19 Suitcases under the seat appear to contain
20 Nothing pressing
21 Interlude for arm and foot
22 Unmoved by the nearly destroyed
23 How keeping an object long enough makes it real

TWO

27 I want to dress like Cal Worthington and hoola hoop across the country somehow in tribute to Peace Pilgrim
28 I took the workaholic
29 While discussing forgiveness
30 The captions of the previous
31 This is the worst.
32 The dictums of nature are all
33 I said, "I'm going to dress up like Elvis soon,"
34 A chance of drizzle aprés—
35 We will do listening exercises every day except Thursday.

36 "Our relationship
37 Changed hair color and over-bright retort
38 In the film, the Queen of the Amazons is
39 My hamstrings are holy and epic.
40 Avoid these facts.
41 I am the father of Kung Fu.

THREE

45 Game Over digital groom and bride T-shirt.
46 Tire of hair to dry, autobiography
47 I heart cities and Europe and can't hear
48 Not careful enough with language.
49 Not careful enough with gesture—
50 Bodies, machines, plants, and the universe

FOUR

53 I am supposed to keep a record throughout the day

FIVE

57 "Are you tired of it yet?"
58 The weather is done with our sanctity.
59 I don't understand you, so I think you're making fun of me.
60 A person who coughs long enough
61 I love now.

SIX

65 From, Blank Stare.
66 Wake up in love
67 Irony/outer voice of critique
68 I'd like to love you at the expense of the poem.

69 Inner vibration object out
70 Forced upon challenge as if employment—
71 Tell me every unexamined emotion.

SEVEN
75 For years I kept a separate account
76 On the bus by young men speaking Portuguese.
77 Not that uncommon southern SoCal
78 Impose one foreign substrate on another—
79 Neglected infrastructure How you live
80 Flat tire—
81 On bad days

EIGHT
85 Fear what sentences can hold fill Draglines marine
86 War makes military personnel throw up.
87 Smell of soaped-over labor exhaustion "Egypt
88 He's a psychologist now
89 Understand Love To interpret the world through
90 I love my girlfriend.

NINE
93 "Extreme California Cheerleading," nearly on the tracks—

CODA
95

ACKNOWLEDGMENTS & ABOUT THE AUTHOR
104

ONE

Today   I objectify   everyone
I see
          stare at their butts   legs   arm muscles   Bump
into them   Sleep   Wake up
      inevitably   irritated

The history of history as naked women   Real women
actually naked   both in the city and the forest
and also in the fields   in all topographies
Pen-less in all topographies

Looking up   excessive gesture
or left out expansion

Too boring to continue   Symptomatic summer
home   What do the Berkshires mean?   Debt
as commercial humor   Market place drives
by and explain about driving   on highways   at night

Lay words on a page sounds like sex

White space as highway

Sit next to someone who doesn't want
Next to

Yes but is this interesting?

The woman in the wig changed
her wig Ask her Tom Varga is
a real estate person who sells real estate Think
TV or Viagra Wake up in a panic
about real estate about not wanting it

A 70s horror movie without the movie   Am all about
the amulet   the ocean bacteria   the old moorings off the state
beach   Deer sign   the real possibility of hitting them and
gulls   and pelicans   cormorants and ducks   possums

A possible possum rescue center!   How the young survive
even if a car crushes their mother's head   if the bus does

they might

The bus driver stops
the bus somewhere
that isn’t a stop   gets out and gives
a sandwich   to the woman managing
the coffee cart
          “I love you”   she says
     This never happens again

Not because of tacos de birria   nauseous
again   Send a box of old dresses   In the mood to miss
you most at sunrise   but I only feel cold
                “It is the glory of God to conceal a thing”
and something about the limited life span   of problems
The glory of distance   too   Today I want everyone   naked

Black Friday shopping death   Any facetime
is better than   happy happy
What to say
land   of   off
The potential to not die today

Suitcases under the seat appear to contain   a bag of potatoes
and a small fire extinguisher   And a woman
with a big plush chicken stuffed animal chicken gets on
and when she gets off she nearly forgets   the chicken
but doesn't   Says   "Oh, mi pollo!"   And next to
a woman "from Texas" where   she says   "people are clean
and polite" and "Mexicans are clean   and polite" and "You look
like you are from Texas" No but say   "Yes I am from Dallas"

Nothing   pressing
on any part   against
any part
Threw up at the holidays
at real estate
at marriage at labor
Nothing
pressing on any part

Interlude for arm and foot for rain A story
might code as an offering I mean
love constructed for love

Like a big rectangular building full of
internal orifices
or the parking lot surrounding it We're looking
for our car We're at IKEA
or IHOP

Unmoved by the nearly destroyed
golf tent   Someone's saying
how bad it is
Thinking of a man
in a coat   maybe the coat of a football team
fan   and jeans with   months of unwashed
wear   And the woman with the plush
chicken   who almost   forgets it again
but she doesn't   She doesn't forget the chicken!
Rehearse   "Señora usted olvidó su pollo"
just in case for the next time

How keeping an object long enough makes it real

TWO

I want to dress like Cal Worthington and hoola hoop across
the country somehow in tribute to Peace Pilgrim.

The rest of this poem is censored.

Or we can just make this the poem / floor plan / teacher.

I took the workaholic
dialog quiz, listened to Texas
country sing “girls, girls girls.”

Someone’s in trouble, but it’s just
the four-bar fiddle solo—
Feel it floating away like the
Anxiety we can’t speak floats in.

“Fuck off,” I said, kind of
an accident to the surfer coming
down a private dock.
He’s said, “Good morning.”

Can not seeing you be our date?

While discussing forgiveness, I got sidetracked and thought about the most recent roadkill—a smashed raccoon in the bicycle lane near the lagoon—and then imagined explaining my forgiveness to a friend who would think it was stupid.

The captions of the previous
commercial stay with the next
and I think, blandly, “Love”
and “How do we say the experience
was rich?” You’re telling me
the story of volunteering
at the rabbit rescue center.

This is the worst.
This worst. That worst.

Maldiction.
Malediction.
Which is it?

The dictums of nature are all
about splinter / I am foreign
but not nearly enough. I'd still
rather be murdered in the city
not the country where the couple
just dies or gets eaten.

I said, “I’m going to dress up like Elvis soon,” and everyone laughed kindly.

A chance of drizzle après—
GOD I AM BORED save me
from fake marble columns.
Assignment deadline
makes a good day to wear red
and we think, "Ha ha.
Is this an OK combination?"
My "I heart public
transportation" shirt
is see-through.

We will do listening exercises every day except Thursday. On Thursday we will watch *The Hills.* And that Jesus camp documentary. I don't know what death is like. How long have you not wanted to get out of bed?

"Our relationship
was about how to be
like frites and pureed
potatoes. It was
enharmonic,
like British
food," she said.

Changed hair color and over-bright retort
dinner table boxout awash in
secrets which are soooooo secret.
Insult withheld here   insert bland
excited comment about landscape.

In the film, the Queen of the Amazons is, incidentally, a vaguely white French-speaking woman being controlled by male ivory smugglers. Later, she leaves her life in the jungle behind for marriage.

My hamstrings are holy and epic.

Substitute the center of you for your belly
and my middle abdominals for your center.
What would be our head? My neighbors
are moving furniture—dropping it—I am
singing to you. It is hard to be sarcastic, but I mean it.

Avoid these facts. Nature as realpolitik: The Phantom Layer is composed of millions of squid and luminous squid ink. Their entire world is known by touch. The Scientists are watching a film that says the sea can feed the world. They, the Scientists, clasp hands, manly-like. Come on, Lady Reporter, the time has come for your promotion, under the sea.

I am the father of Kung Fu. I can't believe it. The conditions are ideal.

THREE

Game Over digital groom and bride T-shirt.

Kind men in high-rise
pants fill up my heart
with job. For I have always
wanted to be a kind man
in high-rise pants
with a steady income
and a cell phone and a long
commute.

The men are etcetera.

Big squid washing up on Oregon beach.

Tire of hair to dry, autobiography
this way then this way then this way:

Artistic people wear scarves
and sometimes baseball hats.

Word as breakfast   rib

Bacteria as daily food chain—you are
the so-and-so who started everything.

Late on the bus   road closure   and

He says he doesn't understand
railroad accidents in California.
He says that where he's from, even drunk
men don't fall asleep
on the railroad tracks.

I heart cities and Europe and can't hear
the grass screaming.
Quiver quiver quiver quiver quiver.

Opaque entrances and exits—   Places to meet or not.

da Da da Da da Da across the plain.

Not careful enough with language. Consider for consistent,
elephant for element, job for joy, god for dog, words for worlds,
filled for field, spilt for split or spilled. Aegean for aegis.

Kid says, "I forgot my mustache." I *hear* him
say it, nearly hit by a car, unhelmeted.

Nausea. Commutes and sun. What yoga says
about repetition and pattern and habit. Sometimes
I throw up every day. Someone says, "Bakersfield."

A field of bakers. Together.

Not careful enough with gesture—How rejecting
something requires loving it   trees, temples, factories, America,
Europe, babies, real estate, genre, parents.

Unless that means that here is home in which case:
Tear/scratch.

Energetic and optimistic
in a way that defies fact. A picture of
you isn't you. A picture of me isn't me.

Lower backache. Head on desk.

Bodies, machines, plants, and the universe
on repeat. The movement
is new but doesn't feel new.

FOUR

I am supposed to keep a record throughout the day of anytime I feel a certain emotion. I am supposed to keep my emotions simple, for example: "glad," "sad," "mad," or "bad." I can also include "afraid" and "guilty." Anytime I feel one of these emotions, I am supposed to note the time of day, the emotion I'm feeling and what was going on when I felt that emotion.

Later, with my partner, trusted friend or therapist, I am supposed to go through my list and share what I've written down. I should try to describe how the emotion felt within my body. I am supposed to talk about how it feels to share my emotional feelings with another person.

FIVE

"Are you tired of it yet?" Can't hear the answer through the waves.

The weather is done with our sanctity. Pacific. California Pacific, precisely. Southern California when the sun leaves. We don't have fingers to count the illnesses, injuries and deaths of people we know. If there were more buses and trains, I'd throw more parties. If you'd throw more parties, I'd take up surfing, be more gracious with small talk. Nothing is discrete—number, person, house, poem—sitting on the balcony as the sun goes by, one bus goes by, not enough people on balconies or buses.

I don't understand you, so I think you're making fun of me. Write until we throw up, or only write at stoplights. I don't understand you, but I see you're anxious for connection. I've forgotten my phone number, my phone.

A person who coughs long enough begins to sound like they're coughing on purpose. Persistent itch. A second, third, fourth or fifth language, almost understood, partially heard.

I love now. Kinds of sleeping and kinds of ritual. Standing on your shoulders was too—

Almost together we're moving with the crowd but no crowds here except in cars. A painting of picnickers looking at greenbelt, airport, and pharmaceutical company—parking lots and ocean beyond.

A whale watching cut free. Watching itself be cut free.

Love naps. Cold mornings and warm ones. An inability not to say "Oh!" when someone says something interesting. Half a nose, clogged, middle backache versus lower backache. Standing on your shoulders, or someone else's shoulders. Falling off them, onto my back, or your back, to a floor without mats, the day before an important holiday or ritual.

So much joy I just might.

SIX

From, Blank Stare. Modern Man's current
address—Wall to wall precarious over
limit texting to share this inexplicable
exaltation: At one point I thought we
would be different from coworkers
peers partners. Many-sided progress
to point to find pleasure in blood, Dostoyevsky.
Mantle of apartments with no mantel
or fire—Look at this. Slip the social. A military
ship used to moor there.

What kind of military ship?
What kind of hawk?

Of street to walk at
night to the club in
shoes that give
us shin splints.

Wake up in love with each other, with the rat on the carpet.

Irony/outer voice of critique as principle affectation—A demonic tendency to marry and divorce, to turn off the new phone. Everyday perversity. Don't eat breakfast until headache, nausea. Breakfast as universal ruin. Hello, solitary bee, where is your hive? A mob of bees at my door. A swarm around the administrative building. Trying to live in an administrative building.

I'd like to love you at the expense of the poem. I'd like a new watch.

Inner vibration   object out   Spinnaker and cormorant
Never expect   to answer the phone   on the beach
Sand makes what kind of a world   Gulls as bears
as government ranger power station
annual replenishment   Some shared abyss   out   places
love   entire continents   the neighbors' horrible music habit
drugs   healthy pelican hatchlings
in the fake lagoon
Stand on California
but the water goes
to Australia and Asia   somewhere you grew
so the water grounds   Grounded as dropping back:
Tops of feet   ankles   shins   quadriceps
lumbar
stomach   lungs
sternum
chest   throat
mouth
eyes
face

Forced upon challenge as if employment—

Choice as choice or street as don't.

Sit on the grass. Travelling along through
landscape and inevitable birds friends fight.

Tell me every unexamined emotion. Sincerity doesn’t matter on the battlefield.

SEVEN

For years I kept a separate account on the Isle of Man.

On the bus by young men speaking Portuguese. Overwhelmed, hungry, swearing whatever. Daily movement ache—Walking but especially not walking. Sitting hurts. Pays. Condos built like adobe, maid uniforms, raw edges for cutting then hemming. The dental hygiene company benefit, petrochemical contracts translated for health, another strange condition.

Not that uncommon southern SoCal

rain

Portuguese could be Brazilian Portuguese

Amazon   you think   Papua New Guinea

Ocean as rainforest green

rain-gray mountains
a partially tame cockatoo   living though old   a copper mine
gold mine   malaria pills   throw up   or hallucinate
Without illness or with it   Nearly   impossible
green and gray rain

earthquakes   mine tailings   dam break

Impose one foreign substrate on another—Detroit as Bucharest, Spain as California, California as Oman. Substitute one wilderness for another—Live in a half-desert but pretend it's just desert-desert and dream of the tropics.

Neglected infrastructure   How you live
exurban   and   carless
Suburb of self   versus
city sewage system   too centralized
to be American   Careless
Perpetual road   repair   Eroding beach
The desert and ocean   are mostly blue
The jungle is mostly green

Flat tire—could be the bus or a pickup truck on a flooded dirt road somewhere. Somewhere is a traffic jam, so you know where you are for now. A man's lolling head sleeping on another man's shoulder—you look for a shoulder, too. She tells you her theory of bus drivers. The ones from the south like to look at bus passes. The ones from the north want you to put them in the machine.

On bad days, imagine the bus is a plane.

EIGHT

Fear what sentences can hold   fill   Draglines marine
sanctuaries   dolphins   salt seaweed   the ocean   Can't
get out of bed   Later greet everyone during the AM
walk   Mollified whistling   "Bless you, bless you"
until it's a swear   The form isn't working
"Next month he turns 88"   When there's no public
life to be separate from   How the   sky   becomes
the   ocean   through   the   cloud

War makes military personnel throw up. Pregnancy makes many women throw up. Even humanitarian operations can induce chronic nausea. He's missing a leg, going to the hospital where the food, he says, is not very good.

Smell of soaped-over labor   exhaustion   “Egypt
killed all their pigs a few months ago”
I remember the story   “There was no scientific basis
for it”   We’re going by a building called
the “Plaza Building” and I want to say something about it
Instead   “How is your fantasy
team doing?”   Coverage   is
good   “Is your wingman ok?”
An F4 flies overhead and drops a sonic boom
on us   We have the F16   It’s rocket
assisted   Imagine what it   does   to your
eyeballs   Who is dispersed?   B52
     We need to extend   Stand

He's a psychologist now, getting residual checks from Universal Studios. An office near the grocery store. It's nice, but he's got to listen to people's problems. "I heard on the radio that San Diego is the fifth most stressed city in our nation after Chicago, Houston, Boston and LA." I want to kiss your post-traumatic stress disorder, then our avatars can go for a jog. Onscreen action powered by a human behind the screen. Breathing in a slow, relaxed way.

Understand   Love   To interpret the world through
rejection—Dancing through the stage

I'm watching Isabelle Adjani as Camille Claudel
and Camille Claudel as herself   Post unwanted abortion

We can hardly function open   I wear my sunglasses on the bus
any message might come along to persuade us

We watched the documentary   about Jonestown
during   our family visit

Most of everyday life is not joyful participation in shared ritual
but the demanding work of dismissing   criticizing

filtering the world with which we come in contact
Couldn't   go   left so I braked to avoid   both door and person

My head is OK but my butt is all scratched up   She was holding
me and I was saying   I'm fine I'm fine I'm fine

I love my girlfriend. We have long term plans, houses, dreams. But, is disdain for Celine Dion innate or learned? Is her ululatory arm-flinging unforgivable? I love you because I imagine that other people find you beautiful. To be aware of it all but not look. As long as life seems to be working, the embedded features of life are working. Conversations pile up.

NINE

“Extreme California cheerleading,” nearly on the tracks—
Open, open! Something happened
in some decade—a different decade than
this one. Something from—Spin. Rip. Foreign
and domestic. With small engines. Somehow this
is still the age of the car, not the plane.
The computer. Not . . . a narrow loss. I’ve underrated
Time, Love, I’m so tired. Something about
Cupid’s arrow becoming fleas or mosquitoes—
how *corazón* is masculine but *open* can be either.
Descriptions and modifiers can be either?
“Outbreak.” No—“Geekstreak.” “Sequoia
Corporate Office.” A mother, son, and—
space aliens. A policeman is
a male siren. Attorney—Atty. Leaning forward while
walking, leaning. Recession retreats at Spa
L’Auberge, coffee and dogs—a piece.
“Keep arm in”—no translation for that. Even marketing
needs to be marketed. Bus waves to bus.
As self—container—possibly a voice. Cabaret.

CODA

Love me up, my am bus says am by love bus,
says me, my, up. Says throw my love up, by me.

Don't bus—am throw—by me, says
up my love. Am think up love, don't throw says me.
Kind bus, don't love, think by me, he says, am throw my
—An he-said. Bus-think. Says: kind-me, throw-by, don't my

Quiver-kind, my he-said. Way. Want quiver. Said he-
kind way. Good quiver-day my want way.

Phone-quiver, good-want, day. Want my supposed
good phone day, just supposed phone good day. My
long supposed just supposed phone. Good just god
long supposed good phone. Open god long just
supposed, can't open god long just know can't open god long.

Can't know person god open. People person know
can't open. Going people person can't know us
going. Know person people water us going, small.

Say small, California. Water-poem. California, say small man-
poem, say California world-man poem. Food world man-
poem, California. Man-watch food-world. Fine-food watch
world, come fine watch food. Come it! Fine watch.

Fine parrot. Come it. Nausea it. Come parrot. Awash
it, parrot nausea, back awash nausea, feel back awash,
feel back—Everyday back-feel isn't everyday, isn't expect
isn't. Fun expect, sir fun expect, nearly fun-sir, nearly cut
sir, cut nearly, understand?

Girls understand cut. Little understand, girls—What
little girls? Little what watching, watching what life, road,
life, watching you're life. You're hair, road, you're walking
hair, hair walking squid. Backache walking—squid! Car
backache. Squid backache. Get car, ritual car.

Get ritual no, working no. Ritual center, working no country, center-
working real center, real country emotion. Green emotion.
Real green emotion-men, green sun. Men hear men, sun
hear share sun. Breakfast hear. Share breakfast, worst breakfast high.

Scientists high times scientists times. Live times stay live, find stay. Listen. Find listen-thing, emotions-thing, leaning-emotions to say sleeping. To say door-sleeping, feeling door gold-feeling. New, new cloud shirt cloud. Shirt-moor work moor. Tell work. Tell chest: bacteria chest—heart bacteria.

Heart, I've leaves. I've heath mantle-time. Night time ways took night, rains took bed Rains bed-face goes face. Goes peers layer peers. Take layer. Take railroad. Europe railroad crowds, it's Europe crowds. It's answer. Answer—ha! Administrative —Ha! Swearing administrative point-swearing, the worst point away. The worst universal, away.

Universal places walk, places arm walk story. Arm baby-story, early pacific. Pacific sea language, language, oh—Oh Beach! Do beach, do bored: grass bored. Grass entire wear.

Wear choice-fill, Thursday—Fill Thursday write. Shared
post. Post-talk, we're wanted ship-landscape. Foreign, foreign
landscape. Speak hot horrible hot, body lower body.

Course lower, break course racing, public racing thought
public. Dinner-thought fake dinner-male business-fake
put business kinds, habit kinds swear. Habit-friends. Swear.
House—friends—house-eat middle. Shoulders middle
free shoulders city free. Felt city.

Drivers felt building drivers building horse.
Ok, horse, ok. Keep cars tired. Heard cars, workaholic heard.
Workaholic partially dress. South dress partially sternum
Headache. Documentary headache.

Avoid documentary. Nice avoid.
Nice. Interesting.
Interesting rain—imagine rain. Imagine wall.
Gray wall, wingman-gray.

Acknowledgments

Earlier versions of "Six," "Seven," and "Nine" appeared in *Eleven Eleven* and in *Ooteoote*'s Vertaallab series. A few versions of "Coda" exist on cards distributed to friends. Many thanks to John Pluecker, Lester Robles O'Connor, Kaitlin Solimine, Anna Joy Springer, and Rae Armantrout who read and commented on the earliest drafts of these poems with attention and kindness; to Adam Deutsch for advice about titles.

The poem on page 90 borrows some language from Sam Anderson, "Taster's Choice," a review of Carl Wilson's *Let's Talk About Love: A Journey to the End of Taste*, in *New York Magazine* (Dec. 17, 2007), http://nymag.com/arts/books/reviews/42082/.

About the Author

K. Lorraine Graham is the author of *Terminal Humming* from Edge Books and *My Little Neoliberal Pony* from Insert Blanc Press. She lives in Washington, DC.

www.ingramcontent.com/pod-product-compliance
Lightning Source LLC
Chambersburg PA
CBHW022116090426
42743CB00008B/878